Triple
Crown

10659433

Bilingual Press/Editorial Bilingüe

General Editor
Gary D. Keller

Managing Editor
Karen S. Van Hooft

Senior Editor
Mary M. Keller

Assistant Editor
David C. Rubí D.

Editorial Board
Juan Goytisolo
Francisco Jiménez
Eduardo Rivera
Severo Sarduy
Mario Vargas Llosa

Editorial Consultants
Tanya Fayen
Gabriela Mahn

Address
Bilingual Review/Press
Hispanic Research Center
Arizona State University
Tempe, Arizona 85287
(602) 965-3867

Triple Crown

*Chicano, Puerto Rican,
and Cuban-American Poetry*

Roberto Durán

Judith Ortiz Cofer

Gustavo Pérez Firmat

Bilingual Press/Editorial Bilingüe
TEMPE, ARIZONA

ISBN: 0-916950-71-9

Library of Congress Catalog Card Number: 87-70081

PRINTED IN THE UNITED STATES OF AMERICA

Cover design by Christopher J. Bidlack

Photo credits: p. 12 and back cover, top left: Craig Barber; p. 64 and back cover, bottom: John Cofer; p. 122 and back cover, top right: Rosa Perelmuter Pérez.

Acknowledgments

This publication is made possible, in part, with public funds from the New York State Council on the Arts and the National Endowment for the Arts, a federal agency.

Judith Ortiz Cofer wishes to express her gratitude to the Florida Fine Arts Council, Division of Cultural Affairs, for a fellowship which permitted her to finish *Reaching for the Mainland*. In addition, she and the editors express their appreciation to the following journals for permission to reprint poems included in this volume:

Kansas Quarterly, for "To My Brother, Lately Missed" and "The Way My Mother Walked," in Vol. 15, No. 1 (1983).

St. Croix Review, for "Woman Watching Sunset" and "A Photograph of Mother at Fifteen Holding Me," in Vol. 15, No. 2 (1982).

Southern Humanities Review, for "Moonlight Performance," in Vol. XVI, No. 3 (Summer 1982; © 1982 by Auburn University), p. 211.

Revista Chicano-Riqueña, for "What the Gypsy Said to Her Children" and "Progress Report to a Dead Father," in *Woman of Her Word: Hispanic Women Write*, ed. Evangelina Vigil (Houston: Arte Público Press, 1983).

(Acknowledgments continue on last page of book.)

Contents

CAROLINA CUBAN, *Gustavo Pérez Firmat*   121

Preface

Triple Crown offers to the reader of serious poetry three full-length collections of poems by three important young poets. Roberto Durán, Judith Ortiz Cofer, and Gustavo Pérez Firmat happen to be, respectively, Chicano, Puerto Rican, and Cuban-American, and thus this anthology provides not only a wealth of poems by three important, emerging young writers, but a sampling of literary perspectives from the three largest and most significant Hispanic communities residing in the continental United States.

Roberto Durán's *Feeling the Red on My Way to the Rose Instead* is broadly and generously Chicano in its content. The relationship between brown and white peoples, the cultural artifacts of Mexican-American popular and occasionally street culture (La Virgen de Guadalupe, tattoos, pintos and la pinta, rosaries, quickie quarters, etc.), community action and community personalities, bugs and butterflies, scars, colors, and other markings of identification, all make their appearance here. On the other hand, Durán's poetic persona and his literary style are highly distinctive, even counter-intuitive. Those Chicano poets who have celebrated, exonerated, exorcised, or otherwise cultivated the pueblo and barrio culture have usually selected epic (e.g., Corky Gonzales), folk (e.g., Raúl Salinas), or "hip" styles (such as the "rant" forms that perhaps stem from Ginsberg and other beat poets). Not so Durán, who is one of the few Chicano poets (Leroy Quintana is another such notable) to express himself in a limpid and lucid, witty, and even epigrammatic form. Strong metaphors, intense feelings, and a highly charged, intellectually provoking content characterize *Feeling the*

Red on My Way to the Rose Instead, which from the formal point
of view makes abundant use of consonance, assonance, alliteration, and overtly formed rhymes (including internal rhymes as
in the title and in "Mr. Dan the Man White"). His poems are
short, they're sharp, and often they hurt. But they hurt good,
rather like the moment when the expert masseuse (not masseur,
in macho Durán's case) touches the raw nerve with just the right
prescription of pressure.

   Judith Ortiz Cofer's *Reaching for the Mainland* is a consummate
work of elasticity. Stretching to her fullest, Ortiz Cofer encompasses the *patria* and *matria* of Puerto Rico as well as the crossedover new continent and all the movements and permutations
in between. She also contributes creatively to the mind-body conundrum that has been the bane of the West. This is a thoughtful
poetry, saturated in the twin ambience of death and desire, classic
in its consideration and weighing in the mind's eye of previously felt situations and events such as a moonlight performance,
old men playing dominoes in the plaza, women watching sunsets,
a praying Margarita, Josefina, María or Isabel. But reductio
ad intellectum is not the point. The mule is pissed off although
it's still loyal. Pissed not only because its eyes no longer see the
rocks but because its old masters are gone and no longer touch
it in friendship, and the new master prods it with contempt. Still
lucid of mind in her calvary, the *madre* yet presses her sharp
fingers into our flesh,

> drawing our mouths to hers,
> breathing death into us and calling us
> her babies.

   Stretching, reaching for the formula (*cantaría, amaría, viviría.* /
Please repeat after me); clearly there is no formula, unless it is
the formula of reaching and stretching, and these are not so much
the results of glowing afterthoughts, but the habit structures of
a (celestial?) body that needs to touch and be touched.

   Gustavo Pérez Firmat affirms himself a *Carolina Cuban* although
elsewhere he says he only resides there; he lives in Miami (Mi

mami). Such an affirmation, if it were miraculous (or at least medieval and homey rather than modern and estranged), could add up to something like a three-in-one miracle, padre, *infans noster*, and the Holy Ghost all residing in one. Pérez Firmat affirms nothing of this order, however: his is the epistemology of the esquizo-paranoid, all maniático mixed up. Where the poet escapes the muddle of the mind as well as "the prison house of language" is in lingual stir-fryery. Let us count the ways: the poet comes up with three (in one). There is English and there is Spanish and the omnipresent *autre* of existential angst. It's a rainbow coalition that achieves an end run around complacent literary conventions that would make a Miami Delfín proud.

What freedom is there, then, for the transculturalized poet? Is the attraction to Cuba really nostalgia or merely curiosity? If you say tomato and I say tu madre (el Huitlacoche once "investigated" this in "Searching for La Real Cosa"), if the fact (as opposed to the pose) is that to write in English falsifies the subject since the subjected doesn't belong in English (though nowhere else), then what freedom for the crazed, stereoscopic poet except in the richly polyglottic registers and rhetorics of his made up (e.g., composed) Spanish and English and their interstice in the *autre*? Rarely has so much been accomplished across languages and the seas.

Feeling, reaching, and babeling. We, the editors of the Press, hope you will enjoy this *Triple Crown*, both its roses and its thorns, as much as we have.

GARY D. KELLER
ARIZONA STATE UNIVERSITY

Feeling the Red on My Way to the Rose Instead

Roberto Durán

Roberto Durán is a product of the Chicano struggles of the 1960s. His works reflect the environment of the fights against the social injustices committed by the haves against the have-nots.

Born in Bakersfield, he lived in Delano, California, until the age of seven. His mother, Lupe Durán, was a single mother who raised her children while working as a farm laborer in the fields of Kern County. Roberto worked in the fields of the Santa Clara Valley to buy clothes and pay for school supplies; he bought his first car by working in a summer program for disadvantaged youth. By 1968 he was involved in the United Farm Workers Organizing Committee, working to support the grape boycott in San José. In 1972 he entered San José City College while continuing his community involvement. In 1974 he completed his first significant collection of poems, a class project that discussed police harassment of Chicanos. On July 4, 1977, in a confrontation with the police, Durán assaulted two officers, trying to prevent them from shooting a friend. He received a four-year sentence to Soledad State Prison. After a year in Soledad, he began to pour out his life through poetry. "I was trying to make sense of my life. Where did I begin to lose aspirations? I wasn't a habitual criminal. I had the qualities to be a successful person. I knew I was a good human being. So why was I here?"

In 1980, immediately upon his release from Soledad, Durán published a chapbook, *A Friend of Sorrow*, doing much of the production himself. In 1985 he graduated from San José State University with a B.S.W. from the School of Social Work. In addition to these accomplishments, he won first place in a poetry competition sponsored by *El Tecolote*, and in recent years he has given numerous readings throughout California, including the 11th International Chicano Latino Teatro Festival (San Francisco, September 1981), the Floricanto Benefit for the San José to Mexico Spiritual Walk (November 1981), the 6th Annual Festival Primaveral of the Fine Arts Commission of San José (March 1981), and the Conference on Barrio Gang Violence, Ventura City College (April 1982).

To Anna and Mom

RED

In the thorns feeling the red
on my way to the rose instead

CHESSMEN

And the bad men of chess
sit on their park benches
as brown fingers silently move
the black and white men
and the checkmate! came
twenty years and ten tattoos too late

TINTA

la tinta   tinta   tinta
pinta   pinta   pinta
el pinto   pinto   pinto

Tattoos

Tattoo madness
terrible pain
permanent ink stain
anywhere will do
of gun towers
and sad flowers
convicts' arms
tales of power
portrayed in
India black ink
tear drop eyes
La Virgen de Guadalupe
proudly displayed
on a young warrior's skin
a barrio's tattoos
are always in

Mom

Remember Mom and the way she sipped
her daily cup
remember Mom never giving up
remember her pacing and racing
worn spotted dotted
miles of kitchen tiles
and still the hard years have not
erased her gentle generous smile

Rosary

Time measured
by a mother's
lonely far away face
she keeps no calendars
as she carries out her silent sentence
brown baked hands clutching
red rosary beads
she prays for stray seeds

Thoughts

My thoughts traveling at the speed of light
jump from peaks of stone when alone

they jump to the cold sea floor
bearing the weight of an ocean once more

RUTHIE'S LUCKY INN

For welfare mothers at Ruthie's Lucky Inn
it's almost a sin not to give in
to pressure from within bullet proof
plexiglass
where six hands are dipped daily
seven days a week even as I speak
so give to Jerry's kids they always say
before one walks away
as young mothers cup
and await shooting silver coins
that cling and clang into their hands
they loom for an instant like giant
granules of shiny sands and back
they go to the man
and yes it is true that some of us
will feel gacho and strange
if we don't give back the change

Cobwebs

I
with a single swipe of my hand
wiped away the delicate tiny strands of cobwebs
that softly swayed above my pale ceiling
it was quite a strange feeling
simply a symbolic frolic
now to destroy those supposed waiting webs
that surrounded me in moments of anguish
how I wish how I wish

Mr. Dan the Man White

Thank your lucky stars
you're not behind death row bars
where countless years flash before
condemned men
so too bad for those without
the name game and fame
these few words are a reminder
of a justice that was kinder
so stop and think of forgotten men
washed down equal justice's
white white sink

WAX LOVE

I love you
never leave me
I'm sorry
always and forever
ours is true love
you're mine
I'm yours
you clean the toilets
I'll scrub the floors
oldies but goodies
capture
rapture
young minds
inspired by
spinning black wax
involving
revolving
around
circular discs

CHANGE THE STATION

A voice interrupts the oldies but goodies radio station
temporarily halting a heart's sweet sensation
as erratic static changes my romantic mood causing me to brood
and in a few swift seconds I listen again as my eyes glisten
off the distant reminiscent planet Venus
a beautiful journey that takes only the flash of an eyelash
and so the message is clear for ears that want to hear
change the station

SOLIDARITY DAY

Solidarity day came and went away
where right leftists protested
and left behind wordy leaflets
pudgy pigeons pitied not politicians that day
in the city by the bay
where solidarity day came and went away

IF

If I were blinded
would I still search
and try and find peace
after knowing the beauty of sight
yet
not attempt to ever see the visual reality of me?

Midnight Moths

Pesky powdery moths
flapping furiously their wings
while dancing insanely
to the incessant rains

mutant butterflies
fighting for each other's space
flying in futility as they race
to a fluorescent dance of death

The Box

The tube of motel cubes
lubes my nerves when day is done
and the sunshine shadow hides in my lampshade
comes the darkness
and worn shoes stick glued to the floor once more
my soles rest best
while staring at flashing figures
of late late shows

all dead now

Silver Hair

My first silver hair
appeared on my beard
it was weird
the way the next day
it disappeared
so much for wisdom

Trendy Categorization

Hispanic
Herpanic
Hispanic
Herpanic
Hispanic
Herpanic
Hispanic
Herpanic
Hispanic
Herpanic
Hispanic
Herpanic
Hispanic

JUST JEANS

jeans jeans jeans
dyed blue blue
sometimes speak to you
in erotic fabric ways
these exotic days
fine lined styled stitch
with men on them
and the libidinal itch

just jeans

Half-Way Harry

Now and then half-way men
walking about town
looking down and around dull grey curbs
where silent secrets surface
the medicated men whisper
while walking to their half-way homes
in a cigarette fret
they walk by headless feet not caring nor wanting to meet
from one side of town to the other they're walking you see
discounted people by you and by me
we are we and they are they and they're o.k.
just keep them away
look! here comes half-way Harry as timid as a mouse
what a shame he never married
watch as he goes conversing to himself
while stepping to his half-way house
and with patience we all wait for the day
half-way Harry goes all the way

HUNGRY EYES

Look!
a hungry baby waits
with an air filled stomach
beautiful round almond eyes
shaded by giant lashes
that hold back monsoon tears

FRIENDLY FIRE

Fire in the eastside of town
neighbors talking once again
after ten years of silence
how quickly fires ignite and excite
the nosey stranger
hot embers and family members
park in the dark and spark spontaneous speech
high school days are remembered on smokey streets

New Menu

In 1968 it was great 1969 was just fine
where were you in 1972?
now it's 1983 and the minority bone has been thrown
for you and for me
as brown burrito stands quickly slickly changed hands
pues ahora es can you guess
Chinese-Vietnamese Cuisine
top too too mean
el menú me and you
are once again new

SUPER FREAK

And the song says do the freak do the super freak
as show-town sneaks into our pockets
meanwhile more South American refugees flee
as once again military men blow off another brother's knees
with government rockets
as they make their way into our cities
escaping the torture and rape
we in America put on our headsets and tape
and the song says do the freak and dig that funky beat

BORED

A crumpled rumpled old man
thumbs through an issue of National Geographic
his hurting hand rubbing thinned gray hair
and his mad mouth grinning while grinding
on bitter ivory
bored
a man silently rages
while thumbing countless pages

COLORED CRAYONS

Yes, I write about crayon-colored folk
I even dare to poke fun at culture
by way of my poetry
and at times it would seem odd
that they would applaud
as a result of an insult

just kidding

WINDOW

The big black crow nervously pecks
his daily meal
acting crow cautious
like paranoid people
at least you can fly away after your fill
and here i'll be still
the crow not sure whether to stay or go
bobs his glistening neck to and fro
fearing even the darting brown sparrow
shooting in like an arrow

just as quickly the crow is gone

COMMUNITY ACTION MEETING

Five guest talkers
four campaign walkers
three broken speakers
two rows of empty seats
and a poem about apathy

WEDDING BAND

Hard timing it
and feeling bold
today I sold
fourteen karats of gold

Sometimes

Sometimes in a fast moving car i'm handsome
and heads turn in lust
other times at stop signs i'm ugly
and the smile is in disgust

Earring

A hole in the ear
is in this year
and not necessarily queer!

S.J.S.U. GUEST LECTURES

Today Stokely Carmichael spoke and joked
where Eldridge Cleaver cleaved his new cleaver
deep into the hearts of the Black Student Union
today Stokely Carmichael did speak
of havoc wreaked by Yankee Capitalism
some students were amused sneered and walked
away confused
so where did you go Third World Brothers
and Sisters? as well dressed Asians
looked the other way that day
Don't wanna hear 'bout Vietnam baby
not one Japanese nigger please
today I shook the hand that shook
and took the amphitheatre audience
today I hugged the man that bugged
students into consciousness
yes Stokely Carmichael's native white attire
caused quite an ire
but didn't tire me
Thank You Kwame Turé

Fine Wines

Let us toast and boast and give thanks to full wino tanks
let us toast and give thanks to the rows and skid rows
of fine wines
as throughout this great grape state dainty stinky pinkies
swing thru the air so suave and debonair
so let us toast to another year for fine wishes
and the quarts of justice

Canned

Memories of Mom
run through my mind
toiling in the burning sun
of the San Joaquin Valley
as I open countless cannery cans
I can't help but think of her backaches all for nothing
after all here I am opening fruit cans
after all

EAST OF EDEN

Military choppers flying constantly overhead
as crop dusters kill bugs dead
in the flourishing fertile Salinas Valley
as barrio youth and old provide jobs
for California's Department of Corrections
they are gathered from East L.A.
to East of Eden
Steinbeck Country
set me free of mice and men
where two-legged rats
are fed to convict cats

Beer Can

Empty beer can
thrown twisted and drained of its power

after having provoked many sighs
and long good-byes

WAIT

Wait and listen for the wild winds come
casting away sins
listen closely those ears distant and deaf
the four-legged creatures know
listening while whistling winds weep
sweeping aside brush and thistle
while nearby church prayers echo through epistles
they too are constant and forever

Poem for Bathroom Poets

Spics don't suck, toothpicks do

Untitled

What's that blond hair doing there in my taco?

Night Is Near

The night is near
and once again I'll become drunk in my aloneness

as my thoughts run rampant fast and furious
while others sleep my mind creeps
into a dammed up wall eager to burst

SCARS

What if wrinkles and scars were beauty marks in reverse

then who would be lucky and who would be cursed?

HAPPY BIRTHDAY

As I glanced at the calendar
for the fifth time
I noticed it was your birthday yesterday
since you forgot mine
I forgot yours too

IMAGES

When you come across Jesus Christ
or the Virgin Mary on paper
do you feel safer
or do you hold it
before you fold it
and think twice before you crunch it?

THE RED SWING

The red swing swings silently now
where my child once laughed

only the memory remains
as seen through water-colored eyes

the swing swings silently now
hypnotizing

LENORE

The beautiful lady Lenore
the fools called her whore
couldn't give no more
now she reads books by the score
her new name is bore
this lovely lady Lenore
never spoken of anymore
what the hell for?

PROTEST

We the people of color y hueros too
don't have to carry boycott cards
or pin buttons in our skins
consequently we do not protest
we are a protest

BACK POCKET

Collection of funeral cards
still fills a moneyless wallet

IN MEMORY OF

I carry their dates of existence
in the back pockets of my mind

WEEDS

The green weeds that grow
in vacant lots
have grown taller than me
they even look pretty

Poster Revolution

¡VIVA CHE!
¡VIVA CHAVEZ!
¡VIVA ZAPATA!
VIVA paper towels
as Taco Bell sells sells sells
as sexy lips and shapely hips
crunch and grind Pancho Villa Chips

POSTER REVOLUTION!

QUICKIE QUARTERS

Quarters fall quickly
into slits and bits of song
juke boxes and various videos are insatiable
but we give and give
quickie quickie quarters

My Enemy

Hate-red eyes scanning
a warning light flashes
lashing lashes slam shut
no I dare not approach you
my instant enemy
you stick knives in me
on sight
will you ever set me free
or is freedom within me?
my enemy
your angry face
merely a reflection
of a revolutionary culture
history repeats
one of us must die
without ever asking why
my friend

Silence

The silence is screaming
hearts cry out
in the immeasurable volume
of suffering men
newborn tears sparkle
angry diamonds
reflect protect the heart

Pent Up

As my hand moved towards
your body
I awakened by feeling smooth
skinned paper

THE I

So forget the I
forget it
for just one minute
step outside if you dare but beware
you might like it

Piece Officers

Have you ever been insulted
by strangers in blue
not sure what to do
to attack or to hold back
have you ever felt hated and despised
has anger ever held you hypnotized
have you ever been pushed
in blood splattered rooms
called everything vile words of hate
that infiltrate the soul of a man
have you ever had your manhood crushed?

BORDER TOWNS

Border towns and brown frowns
and the signs say
get back wet back
souls are searched at night by silver flashlights
gringos and greasers play cat and mouse
and I still wonder why
do apple pies lie?
the signs say live the american way
visit but don't stay
be a friendly neighboor hire good cheap labor
as rows and rows of illegal star war aliens
are aligned and maligned
as the morning shouts fill the morning chill and still
they will not
no way José go away

BEAUTIFUL STRANGER

500 camel packs
surround your sexy face
every piece intricately placed
8 by 10 stranger
carefully torn off magazine cover
my beautiful stranger
fills an empty frame
and taunts
an empty heart
help me do my time
and play my love game
with me

CAPTURED

I kicked the shields
of my resistance the plastic
police barrier
piece of segregation where intoxicated
profanities still echo
in the back seats of my mind
in the spaces between the blue and brown
ignorance abounds
you handcuffed my hands yet I still
fought you
with my feet as the black batons beat
and both sides have lied consequently denied
any wrongdoing

Color

Excuse me white
off-white pale america
in my search and journeys
of my brown life
on blue green planet earth

Reaching for the Mainland

Judith Ortiz Cofer

Judith Ortiz Cofer was born in Puerto Rico in 1952. As the daughter of a career Navy man, she traveled with her family from the Island to the United States regularly during her childhood. Paterson, New Jersey, eventually became their home base, and there she attended Catholic schools and learned the English language. She earned an M.A. in English at Florida Atlantic University, where she was awarded a scholarship for graduate work at Oxford University by the English Speaking Union of America. In 1981, the Fine Arts Council of Florida selected her as a recipient of a fellowship in poetry. She has won two scholarships to the Bread Loaf Writers' Conference, serving on the administrative staff for three years.

At present, Judith Ortiz Cofer lives in Athens, Georgia, with her husband and daughter and works at the University of Georgia as an Instructor of English. Her work has appeared in numerous journals including *Prairie Schooner, Kansas Quarterly, New Letters, Southern Poetry Review, Bilingual Review, Southern Humanities Review*, and others. As first place winner of the 1985 Riverstone International Poetry Chapbook Competition, her entry, *Peregrina*, was published by the Foothills Art Center of Golden, Colorado, in 1986.

To John and Tanya,
y a mi madre,
Fanny Morot Ortiz

The Birthplace

THEY SAY

They say
when I arrived,
traveling light,
the women who waited
plugged
the cracks in the walls
with rags
dipped in alcohol
to keep drafts and demons out.
Candles were lit
to the Virgin.
They say
Mother's breath
kept blowing them out
right and left.
When I slipped
into their hands
the room was in shadows.
They say
I nearly turned away,
undoing
the hasty knot of my umbilicus.
They say
my urge to bleed
told them I was like a balloon
with a leak,
a soul trying to fly away
through the cracks in the wall.
The midwife sewed
and the women prayed
as they fitted
me for life
in a tight corset of gauze.

But their prayers
held me back,
the bandages held me in,
and all that night
they dipped
their bloody rags.
They say
Mother slept through it all,
blowing out
candles
with her breath.

The Woman Who Was Left at the Altar

She calls her shadow Juan,
looking back often as she walks.
She has grown fat, her breasts huge
as reservoirs. She once opened her blouse
in church to show the silent town
what a plentiful mother she could be.
Since her old mother died, buried in black,
she lives alone.
Out of the lace she made curtains for her room,
doilies out of the veil. They are now
yellow as malaria.
She hangs live chickens from her waist to sell,
walks to town swinging her skirts of flesh.
She doesn't speak to anyone. Dogs follow
the scent of blood to be shed. In their hungry,
yellow eyes she sees his face. She takes him
to the knife time after time.

HOUSEPAINTER

The flecks are deeply etched into
the creases of his fingers and
the paint will not wash off.
It was a hilltop house he painted last
for an old woman going blind
who wanted it to blend into the sky.
It took him two weeks working alone,
and the blue, a hue too dark, stood out
against the horizon like a storm cloud,
but since clouds had also gathered over her eyes,
she never knew.
He explained his life to me,
a child on my grandfather's lap concerned with his
speckled hands only because they kept me
from my treasure hunting in his painter's shed
where cans on shelves spilled enamel over their
lids like tears running down a clown's face.

LA TRISTEZA

Books. By reading them,
by writing them, he thinks he has escaped
the sadness of his race.
When he returns to the old town,
open like a violated tomb, bleached bones
exposed to the sun, he walks bareheaded
among the people, to show his disdain
for the sombrero, the hat that humbles.
He has grown somber and pale
in the New England winter, ashamed
of the mahogany skin, the yellow teeth
of the men who move slow as iguanas
in the desert. When they greet him,
their eyes roll up to heaven, each claiming
to have been his father's most intimate friend.
Here they never let go of their dead.
And the women, timid blackbirds, lower
their eyes in his presence.
Damn the humility of the poor that keeps them
eating dust. He thinks this, even as he takes
the girl with skin supple as suede to his hotel
where her body spreading under him is a dark stain
on the clean white sheets he has earned.

Moonlight Performance

The pond opens up to the hill
like a woman's vanity mirror.
The naked figure poised on a branch
overhanging the water steps into the moonlight;
he sees lights like a maniac's eyes darting
through the trees playing
frenzied peek-a-boo with him.
As the train rounds the last corner,
he can make out dozens of faces peering
into the night
supplying him with a moving audience,
the engine, with the music and thunder
necessary for a feat of daring.
He bounces and leaps as the headlight
suspends him in space,
completing the performance.

On the Island I Have Seen

Men cutting cane under a sun relentless
as an overseer with a quota,
measuring their days
with each swing of their machetes,
mixing their sweat with the sugar
destined to sweeten half a continent's coffee.

Old men playing dominoes in the plazas
cooled by the flutter of palms,
divining from the ivory pieces
that clack like their bones, the future
of the children who pass by on their way to school,
ducklings following the bobbing beak
of the starched nun who leads them in silence.

Women in black dresses keeping all the holy days,
asking the priest in dark confessionals
what to do about the anger in their sons' eyes.
Sometimes their prayers are answered
and the young men take their places
atop the stacked wedding cakes.
The ones who are lost to God and mothers
may take to the fields, the dry fields,
where a man learns the danger of words,
where even a curse can start a fire.

THE MULE

I have been loyal for too long.
My master is gone, and his son
gazes at me with the eyes of a stranger.
He does not touch me in friendship but
prods me in contempt,
and I must carry his burdens joylessly
up and down this mountainside.
My eyes no longer see the rocks
in my path as clearly,
yet each step takes me closer
to the place I have chosen
on a perfect and unyielding road,
no matter who leads.

The Man Who Lost His Handwriting

There are some who remember Andrés
when he still had words. In my mother's day
he was town scribe, directing every event
with pen and ink.
Legends arose that Don Andrés
was touched by God. Women came to him
before naming their children, searching
his letters like the tarot for symbols. My aunt
was christened Clorinda del Carmen because he gave
the C's the wings of an angel. Andrés also sealed deaths
with his eternal black ink. Don Gonzalo,
the priest, had been heard to say
that even Saint Peter would be pleased to let
a soul into paradise with such a pass.

It was words, they say, that broke Andrés. Two wars
in two decades, reams of telegrams to transcribe from blue
to black; all the letters he had written for the town's sons
stacked on his desk like a tombstone.
Until letter by letter, he lost his alphabet. In time,
he forgot the location of his office.

Andrés now scans the streets like a black periscope
for the bright things he collects:
Foil, glass, nails—anything
that catches the sun.
When he finds what he needs,
he files it away in its proper pocket.

WOMAN WATCHING SUNSET

Sitting on the steps of her clapboard house
she has only to lift her eyes
to encompass all of her world,
as familiar to her as her own reflection.
The clothes on the line sway
to the wind's whispered waltz,
the dog lies limp in the shade,
one paw throbbing in dream pursuit,
the begonias bordering her porch sway in their clay pots
like girls waiting to be asked to dance under the
shadow of an ancient oak leaning over them
like a bored chaperone.
This is the best time, when her corner of God's earth
is held in the fingertips of the retreating sun.
And tomorrow she will create her world again,
from scratch.

GRACE STANDS IN LINE FOR SATURDAY CONFESSION

I have knelt to them,
pressing my breasts hard against
their confessional walls.
I have issued them the challenge
of my mortal sins,
imagining them bound
to my secret voice.
I have watched their moist fingers slip
from bead to bead
on their worn-down-to-the-wood rosaries,
and I have listened to the heavy sighs
of their unctuous absolutions.
I have dared to remind them of the darkness
in the cathedral, the pungency of flesh,
that no scented candle can conceal.

WHAT THE GYPSY SAID TO HER CHILDREN

We are like the dead,
invisible to those who do not
want to see,
and our only protection against
the killing silence of their eyes is color:
the crimson of our tents pitched
like a scream
in the fields of our foes,
the amber of our fires
where we gather to lift our voices
in the purple lament of our songs.
And beyond the scope of their senses
where all colors blend into one,
we will build our cities of light,
we will carve them
out of the granite of their hatred,
with our own brown hands.

Pueblo Waking

Roosters call their blood back
from claws wrapped around a post, the dog
stretched under the mango tree stirs
dust into the sunlight as he rises, tin roofs
clamor under the first wave of heat like teapots.
Windows thrown wide, voices are tossed back
and forth, picking up talk where it was
interrupted by the night.
At seven, the church bells sound hollow
after their long silence. Old women in black veils climb
the church steps in single file, like a trail
of worker ants.
                        In August, penitents travel
from all parts of the island to this pueblo
to drag bloody knees up two hundred steps
hewn out of a hillside to the shrine
of the Black Virgin, La Monserrate.
At her feet they leave jewelry and bolts of cloth
for the sisters to make vestments. Many of the
pilgrims have dreams after their visits — numbers and
colors to decipher during the year.
                        But on this day,
Christ's Mother's name is a lament over the late hour,
a plea to hurry to work, to school, or to the store
for *la leche*. Noise rises like an approaching train
until the morning goes round the bend
in a complication of smells,
black beans boiling over the coffee's last call,
and the midday sun begins to wrap the pueblo
in the silence of siesta.

VISITING LA ABUELA

Called in early to soak the day's play from my skin,
slick as a newborn calf, to slip into my crinolines,
in my pink parachute dress, to descend on La Abuela,
who once a month waited for her generations to come listen.
In her incense-sweet room, we'd sip cocoa,
sitting straight-backed on a sofa that insisted we sink.
I'd watch the old woman's hands, folded like fledgling
sparrows on her lap, swoop up to tuck a curl under her cap,
and drop again as if too weak to fly for long.
We'd listen to her tales, complex as cobwebs, until,
at a sign from Mother, who paid these visits like giving alms,
I'd kiss the cheek lined like a map to another time,
and grasping Mother's steady hand,
I'd rush us out into the sunlight.

The Gusano of Puerto Rico

Earthworm, orange as a sunset
over the brown hills of this island,
you surface for food only to become
the tender treat of yellow ants
who climb your back
as you bend your head like a servile camel
to their stings.
Curled around your soft middle,
eyes buried in your body's spiral,
you know your end.
You assume the pose of martyr, but deep
in the warm mud you have left your plentiful,
wriggling seed — more gusanos than mandibles
can crush, opening their eyes in the dark,
without knowledge of sky and sun,
but with the mortal need to seek the light.

THE FRUIT VENDOR

A skeletal man pushing a cart
bright as a carnival, one-eared Gacho
winds his way through town.
Children follow his red and blue hand-wagon,
trying to grab the brass bells on a rope,
mocking his high-pitched call
of *frutas hoy, y viandas*.
Once he had been a player of stringed instruments
but lost his left ear and hand to the swing
of a man's machete over a woman's choice of songs.

The matron in a stained smock
who now moves slow to his call, belly swollen
by childbirth, was courted in her youth
to Gacho's boleros.

At each stop he changes the arrangement:
finding the ripest fruit, he places it on top,
the spiny breadfruits chaperone the tiny bananas,
the green plantains are soldiers on leave
surrounding the blushing mangoes. Then he stands back
and waits for the women to arrive like the despoiling army,
ignoring the harmony of his design
with their random selections.

THE SOURCE

Framed in the doorway of her clapboard house,
Vieja sits in her cane rocker waiting
for the coffee trees to rise to her sight
like red-eyed soldiers startled by the sun's reveille,
and this world-wake belongs to her.

Early shadows condense to reveal a flamboyant tree
heavy with blossoms, leaning over the well
that helped her nurse her generations,
and her progeny have been like the sunflower
rather than the rose, scattering their seed.

Yet it all remains fast on this hill,
this house, the well, herself gathering memories
like grandchildren to her lap, to watch the day
climb the hill like her man did so many seasons ago,
bringing the night on his clothes and on his hands.

LETTER FROM A CARIBBEAN ISLAND

This island is a fat whore lolling
tremulous and passive in the lukewarm sea.
Nature has shamed us like a voluptuous daughter:
no place to hide from the debauchery
of sun, wind and vegetation.
All roads end in the sea,
and the mountains are like a garment
shrunk by the heat.
We are hungry for white, longing for snow.
So much color corrupts the soul.
We pray for a different weather, a civil storm,
one that won't enter our homes
like a soldier drunk on blood.
How can we be good Christians here?
In this tropical Eden we sleep on beds
soaked in sweat and spend our days
under a demanding sun that saps
our good intentions.
There are no puritans here.
We throw open our windows to conceive,
letting the western wind blow life into the seed.
Sinners all, we pass the time as best we can
in paradise, waiting for the bridge across the water.

THE BIRTHPLACE

There is no danger now
that these featureless hills will hold me.
That church sitting on the highest one like
a great hen spreading her marble wings
over the penitent houses does not beckon to me.
This dusty road under my feet is like
any other I have traveled,
it leads only to other roads.
Towns everywhere are the same when shadows thicken.
Yet, each window casting a square of light,
that grassy plain under a weighted sky turning to plum,
tell me that as surely as my dreams are mine,
I must be home.

The Crossing

"Solitude lies at the lowest depth of the
human condition. Man is the only being
who feels himself to be alone and the only
one who is searching for the Other."
— Octavio Paz

MOTHER DANCING IN THE DARK

(And Father somewhere in the Pacific).
She places the needle gently into the worn groove
and a Mexican tenor strains over the violins,
Bésame, bésame mucho . . .
a Mariachi band backs up his demand,
as Mother sinks into the sofa.
From our bed where she has left me
moored to a dreamless sleep, I watch her
rise over her black skirt
like the ballerina in my lacquered music-box,
Como si fuera esta noche la última vez . . .
lift her cheek to a phantom kiss,
Que tengo miedo perderte, bésame, bésame mucho . . .
then bound to the refrain she turns, turns into the shadows
where she is lost to my sight.
(And Father somewhere in the Pacific.)

CROSSINGS

Step on a crack.
In a city of concrete it is impossible
to avoid disaster indefinitely.
You spend your life peering
downward, looking for flaws,
but each day more and more fissures
crisscross your path, and like the lines
on your palms, they mean something
you cannot decipher.
Finally, you must choose between
standing still in the one solid spot you
have found, or you keep moving
and take the risk:
Break your mother's back.

MY FATHER IN THE NAVY

Stiff and immaculate
in the white cloth of his uniform
and a round cap on his head like a halo,
he was an apparition on leave from a shadow-world
and only flesh and blood when he rose from below
the waterline where he kept watch over the engines
and dials making sure the ship parted the waters
on a straight course.
Mother, Brother and I kept vigil
on the nights and dawns of his arrivals,
watching the corner beyond the neon sign of a quasar
for the flash of white, our father like an angel
heralding a new day.
His homecomings were the verses
we composed over the years making up
the siren's song that kept him coming back
from the bellies of iron whales
and into our nights
like the evening prayer.

Arrival

When we arrived, we were expelled
like fetuses
from the warm belly of an airplane.
Shocked by the cold,
we held hands as we skidded
like new colts on the unfamiliar ice.
We waited winter in a room sealed
by our strangeness.
Watching the shifting tale of the streets,
our urge to fly toward the sun
etched in nailprints like tiny wings
in the grey plaster of the windowsill,
we hoped all the while
that lost in the city's monochrome
there were colors we couldn't yet see.

LATIN WOMEN PRAY

Latin women pray
in incense sweet churches;
they pray in Spanish to an Anglo God
with a Jewish heritage.

And this Great White Father,
imperturbable on His marble pedestal,
looks down upon His brown daughters,
votive candles shining like lust
in His all seeing eyes,
unmoved by their persistent prayers.

Yet year after year
before His image they kneel,
Margarita, Josefina, María and Isabel,
all fervently hoping
that if not omnipotent,
at least He be bilingual.

THE WAY MY MOTHER WALKED

She always wore an amulet on a gold chain,
an ebony fist
to protect her from the evil eye of envy
and the lust of men.
She was the gypsy queen of Market Street,
shuttling her caramel-candy body past
the blind window of the Jewish tailor
who did not lift his gaze,
the morse code of her stiletto heels sending
their Mayday-but-do-not-approach into
the darkened doorways where eyes
hung like mobiles in the breeze.
Alleys
made her grasp my hand teaching me
the braille of her anxiety.
The two flights to our apartment were her holy ascension
to a sanctuary from strangers where evil
could not follow on its caterpillar feet and where
her needs and her fears could be put away
like matching towels on a shelf.

SCHOOLYARD MAGIC

Leaning on the chainlink fence of P.S. No. 11,
my flesh cracking in the bitter breeze of a December day,
I burrow deep into my clothes and watch the black girls
jump rope so fast and hot my own skin responds.
Red, green, tartan coats balloon up around
longstem legs, making them exotic flowers and birds.
They sing a song to the beat of the slap-slap
of a clothesline on concrete:

> *A sailor went to sea, sea, sea,*
> *To see what he could see, see, see,*
> *And all that he could see, see, see,*
> *Was the bottom of the deep blue*
> *Sea, sea, sea . . .*

The brick building framing their play,
the rusted fire-escape hanging over their heads,
the black smoke winding above in spirals—
all of it is wished away,
as I let my blood answer the summons of their song,
drawing my hands free from all my winter folds,
I clap until my palms turn red,
joining my voice to theirs,
rising higher than I ever dared.

CLAIMS

Last time I saw her, Grandmother
had grown seamed as a Bedouin tent.
She had claimed the right
to sleep alone, to own
her nights, to never bear
the weight of sex again nor to accept
its gift of comfort, for the luxury
of stretching her bones.
She'd carried eight children,
three had sunk in her belly, *náufragos*
she called them, shipwrecked babies
drowned in her black waters.
Children are made in the night and
steal your days
for the rest of your life, amen. She said this
to each of her daughters in turn. Once she had made a pact
with man and nature and kept it. Now like the sea,
she is claiming back her territory.

A Photograph of Mother at Fifteen Holding Me

Still honey-melon round
from recent motherhood,
she holds me, a limp thing,
away from her,
like children hold their baby dolls,
smiling down shyly
at her amazing deed.
The dark arms look strong,
not too long away
from playground volleyball.
Her white wedgies face each other
in pigeon-toed uncertainty.

WALKING TO CHURCH

Latin girls don't just walk,
they sway sensuously
to the rhythm
of some secret melody.

Demure as sidewalk Mona Lisas,
eyes cast downward
in mocking modesty
from passersby, attempting to conceal
any intimation of the sudden surges
of their adolescent hearts
that put such spring into their steps.

Moving just behind them
all in black is Mamá,
silent, somber sentinel,
also swaying,
a secret song also
playing
on her mind.

"En mis ojos no hay dias"

from Borges' poem
"The Keeper of the Books"

Back before the fire burned behind his eyes
in the blast furnace which finally consumed him,
Father told us about the reign of little terrors
of his childhood, beginning
at birth with his father who cursed him
for being the twelfth and the fairest,
too blond and pretty to be from his loins,
so he named him the priest's pauper son.
Father said the old man kept
a mule for labor
wine in his cellar
a horse for sport
a mistress in town
and a wife to bear him daughters
to send to church
to pray for his soul
and sons
to send to the fields
to cut the cane
and raise the money
to buy his rum.
He was only ten when he saw his father
split a man in two with his machete
and walk away proud to have rescued his honor
like a true hombre.
Father always wrapped these tales
in the tissue paper of his humor
and we'd listen at his knees,
rapt, warm and safe
in the blanket of his caring.
But he himself could not be saved.

To this day his friends still ask,
"What on earth drove him mad?"
Remembering Prince Hamlet I reply,
"Nothing on earth,"
but no one listens to ghost stories anymore.

MEMORY OF LA ABUELA

My grandfather tells me
about the first time he saw her,
a brown figure against the sun,
skirt held up as if beginning
a dance, carrying her shoes
in one hand as she crossed her father's pasture,
pausing now and then
to pick a wildflower.
Ending the anecdote, the old man
lowers his eyes and falls deep into silence,
perhaps seeing a young woman gather her skirts
in a green pasture. In the next telling,
she dances.

MEDITATION ON MY HANDS

They are always folding on each other,
scared pink mice or marsupial embryos
seeking a teat.
Your fingers, Mother, were a vise
strong and quick with the sure grip
of the blind,
always finding the tender spot on my
arm to pinch when I had said too much
in front of the company.
But to be fair,
I would never have been a dropped baby,
though your embrace left me marked
with long tapering stripes.
Mother, with those talented hands,
you should have been a pianist, or one
of those Borgia women who strangled
their unfaithful lovers with fingers
like silk threads.

SHE HAS BEEN A LONG TIME DYING

Skin like a crushed paper bag
and a voice like a shovel striking dry ground,
she calls us to come closer as she rises on her elbows
like some skinny bird poised for flight.
We file past her in generations,
looking her over like a museum piece we fear to touch;
smelling the decay, we try to rush
but she will not let go,
pressing her sharp fingers into our flesh,
drawing our mouths to hers,
breathing death into us and calling us
her babies.

Treasure

It is a sun-blanched day.
His face rises pale as a September moon
over the black suit.
He sits straight-backed on a cement block.
In the background white curtains billow like wings
over his shoulders, or like a summons
to a cool interior. But he is solid against
their movement, staring through
squinting lids past the camera to the field
he would soon harvest, or into the future
at a grandchild he did not live to know, who
has lately found his familiar face glued to the lid
of an old jewelry box, enduring like Spanish gold
among the gaudy trinkets.

The Habit of Movement

THE OTHER

A sloe-eyed dark woman shadows me.
In the morning she sings
Spanish love songs in a high
falsetto, filling my shower stall
with echoes.
She is by my side
in front of the mirror as I slip
into my tailored skirt and she
into her red cotton dress.
She shakes out her black mane as I
run a comb through my closely cropped cap.
Her mouth is like a red bull's eye
daring me.
Everywhere I go I must
make room for her; she crowds me
in elevators where others wonder
at all the space I need.
At night her weight tips my bed, and
it is her wild dreams that run rampant
through my head exhausting me. Her heartbeats,
like dozens of spiders carrying the poison
of her restlessness,
drag their countless legs
over my bare flesh.

Room at the Empire

It is the hour of the exodus.
From my hotel window I watch the biography
of this day unfold: Two women cross 63rd, burdens
on their arms — on their shoulders they carry
the skins of animals.
In step they enter the delicatessen
where they will meet others of their kind.
Slouched in a doorway a drunk lies unconscious, his boots
jutting up like stone markers in the path of pedestrians.
A couple kiss as they wait for "Walk," a crowd gathers
behind the two, who part faces and join hands.
As in an old newsreel they all move forward at once,
dispersing when they reach the other side.
The drunkard stretches, yawning: The rush is over.
Soon the sun pales, a movie screen before the credits,
and in the gathering mist above Lincoln Center
points of light begin to flicker.
Yellow taxis cruise the boulevard like frantic bees
pollinating the city.
The evening drifts away in waves of traffic.
In the new silence I find
I have tuned my breathing to bells of a distant cathedral.

102 Judith Ortiz Cofer

To My Brother, Lately Missed

Crustaceans from the same waters, we
keep our vessels separate though
the currents have flowed in our way more
often these seasons.

And, as time softens the walls between
our chambers,
the echoes of your life sounds have touched me,
but I, concentrating on my pearl, have chosen
the seclusion of my species.

The moon determines your directions now, brother,
while I remain imbedded
in coral, hoarding my treasure in
the silence of a multitude, alone
in this tenement of captives.

LOST ANGELS

for Luis Rafael Sánchez

You may find them in the grey mist
that rises from city sidewalks,
near piles of trash,
like discarded Christmas ornaments.
I have seen them on the frozen clotheslines
of tenements, masquerading
as the long-sleeved shirts of working men
arm-in-arm in a dozen dingy crucifixions,
in the globes of breath
of the park-bench wino sleeping,
in the pink spittle that clings
to his chin like death.
Look for them in the stained plaster
above the insomniac's bed.
It's possible to see them swimming
like a mote in the eyes of a friend
you haven't seen for some time,
who tells you she has heard the wind
calling her name,
who speaks recklessly of the proximity of clouds.

CLOSED CASKET

> "I wake to sleep, and take my waking slow."
> — Theodore Roethke

The bed you slept on was never large enough
for your restless sleep, Father.
After a twelve-to-six shift it was fun
to watch you count down into exhaustion
in starts and jerks as if some mad marionettist
were pulling your limbs with invisible strings.
How does it feel to be sleeping on
this narrow bed?
They have closed the door on you
who never needed privacy to sleep;
you, who took your sleep in boxer's rounds,
waking with glazed and swollen eyes
to an alarm I never heard
no matter how hard I listened.

WE ARE ALL CARRIERS

Now don't think my opinions on this matter are final,
but I believe that we are all
born equipped with a gland of madness,
though its exact location is still unknown;
it hangs in the vault of our skulls
like a pendulum marking time,
thin-skinned like a grape
and popping full of black bile.
In some people it grows into their flesh like
an embryo or a tumor,
in others it swings by a thread exposed
so that a sudden jar or playful shove,
a shrill note or blinding light, will rupture
the delicate membrane causing poison to pour out like
India ink seeping into the brain and
burning away at memory and choice.
From such accidents are snipers made,
and heroes of war.
Most often, though, the damage is minor:
a pinprick leak, slow and almost imperceptible
like the waterdrop that bores a hole into the rock,
accounts for those of us who tread lightly
as we cross the bamboo bridges our enemy
has built in our path,
those of us who daily waver
between writing a poem and slashing our wrists.

In Yucatan

1

Here all day it is high noon, sun baking people
the color of clay. At Uxmal and Chichén-Itzá I have seen
the profiles of an ancient race carved on the golden sandstone
of pyramids; at the hotel in Mérida I see them again, the faces
of desk clerk, bellhop and maid. The woman who makes my bed
bends like a priest over the sacrificial altar; the clay figure
of Chac-Mool, the god of rain, sits on the dresser, gazing
at the nape of her neck where she has wound a braid
into a symbol of eternity. Ending her labors she turns
and I see the Mayan features carved in angles on the solar plains,
the calendar stone, of a face certain in the knowledge of its past.
"Es todo, Señora," she says. It is all.

2

Kukulcán crawls. Quetzalcóatl calls. The serpent gods rule time.
The Toh bird keeps time with its tufted tail swinging
like a metronome. The Maya knew time, giving each day
a name for centuries past their own fall, which they saw
as clearly as the stars each night reflected on a golden water bowl.
The church bells of Mérida call; the Maya also knew the tongue
of bells. From the window I watch a beggar drag his reluctant legs
across the cobblestone to the church steps. The women sweep
by him, a flock of doves in their rebozos. "Caridad,
por Dios, caridad," he calls waving his cane, scattering them.

3

At dusk the men come in from the fields where from
light to dark they have arced the rows of the henequen
plant in the same pendulum motion their ancestors used.
Civilization is a habit.

At day's end they will enter their clay huts, dank
as caverns when Chac sends the rains, to eat the good
maize, watch the world through the flickering magic
of the televisions, and finally sleep in hammocks
made from the hemp they have harvested.
Time is a serpent that circles the world.
Once upon a time men the color of clay saw the coming
of men pale as death, pale as the moon that hangs distant
and mute over all of us, this night in Yucatán.

RETURNING FROM THE MAYAN RUINS

On a night thick with the smells of a recent rain,
I drive through an Indian village where lights
from the round clay huts called chozas make it seem
like a jack-o-latern town where for the stranger driving
through every night is Halloween.
I inhale the air weighted with smells of the damp earth,
the ripe carcass of a dog I swerve to miss, smouldering
heaps of rubbish at every unexpected bend.
Passing an open doorway I glimpse a family sleeping
in layers, each body cocooned in the webbing of a hammock;
nearest the road is the woman whose braid falls to the dirt
floor like a black rope, on her breast an infant suckles.
Shifting to a more silent gear, I leave these new Mayas swaying
ceaselessly to the movement of the earth, suspended
in a deeper sleep than their ancestors could have known.

POSTCARD FROM A FOREIGN COUNTRY

So much left out of the picture.
See the little houses gathered
around the cathedral like girls
making their First Communion,
notice how the old church leans
toward the town as if listening
to its whispered confessions.
They say the mortar is crumbling
under the stones.
I am standing in the church's shadow
as I write you this note,
a shadow it has thrown
on this town for centuries,
watching the night erase this scene
like a drawing on a blackboard,
a message scribbled hastily:
only postcard days are forever.

WHEN YOU COME TO MY FUNERAL

for Betty Owen

Bring conga drums and maracas,
meet at the statue in the plaza,
the one of Columbus pointing his index finger at the sky
as if to say, "you have found your way, amigos."
Be there at 3 o'clock, the hour of the siesta,
when the aroma of perking coffee draws laborers
from the fields to the cool shade
of kitchen and cantinas.

Bring your music and board the bus that goes
to the shore where I always wanted to live.
The trail is treacherous and narrow and the driver
will curse the day and embrace the wheel with
his strong brown arms; he was my friend,
invite him down for the party.

There will be rum-punch and pasteles,
and if you bring a sad word for me leave it on the porch
like a wet umbrella, or better still, toss it out to sea.
I will be among you gathered at the edge of the Atlantic
to compose a new kind of dirge, one of vigorous beat
and a rocking cadence,
one that will take me out like a favorable current,
into the silence of my new way.

STREET PEOPLE

Miami, 1983

In the mornings you see them
sucked like leeches to the walls
of public buildings, hanging on
against the gale storm
of a night on the streets.
They speak to us
with their bodies' occupation
of pestilence, death
by osmosis, the contagion
of dispossession.
If we must pass them, we brace
ourselves with indifference.
It clings to us like the odor
of garlic. We walk fast,
each of us holding tight
to whatever we most fear to lose.

Because My Mother Burned Her Legs in a Freak Accident

I am flying south over the Atlantic
toward one of those islands
arranged like shoes on a blue carpet.
She lies in bed waiting for the balm
of my presence, her poor legs pink
as plucked hens. When her gas stove exploded
as she bent over her soup, the flame grabbed
her ankles like a child throwing a tantrum.
So she has summoned me transatlantically,
her voice sounding singed as if the fire
had burned her from within.
She wants me there to resurrect her flesh,
to reverse time, to remind her of the elastic
skin that once sustained me.
She wants me to come home and save her,
as only a child who has been forgotten and forgiven can.

Progress Report to a Dead Father

"Keep it simple, keep it short,"
you'd say to me, "Get to the point,"
when the hoard of words I had stored for you
like bits of bright tinsel in a squirrel's nest
distracted you from the simple "I love you"
that stayed at tongue-tip.

Father, I am no more succinct now than when
you were alive; the years have added reams
to my forever manuscript.
Lists rile me now in your stead,
labeled "things to do today" and
"do not forget," lists of things
I will never do, lists that I write
to remind me that I can never forget.

I can still hear you say,
"A place for everything and
everything in its place."
But chaos is my roommate now, Father,
and he entertains often.

Simplicity is for the strong-hearted,
you proved that with your brief
but thorough life. Your days were stacked
like clean shirts in a drawer.
Death was the point you drove home
the day your car met the wall,
your forehead split in two, not in your familiar frown,
but forever — a clean break.
"It was quick," the doctor said, "He didn't feel a thing."

It was not your fault that love could not be
so easily put in its right place
where I could find it when I needed it,
as the rest of your things, Father.

Baptism at La Mision

"José Juan Pablo González, I anoint you
in the name of all that's holy,
a Christian and one of us."
I hold him high above the ecstatic crowd
in consecration, and he screams in terror
of space. Longing for solitude
and darkness, he hates the drowning and
the hands, the grinning faces,
the voices singing praises.
He wants only to suck his toes,
and wrap his mother's flesh around him.

FEVER

My daughter is burning and may
burst into flames
before night's end.
Pressing her limp fingers to my palm
I will them to curl,
but reflex has been left
on the other side of the hot door.
Fear touches the nape of my neck,
making me reach back through time,
absorbing child into flesh,
to cool her in my waters.

A POEM

I wish I could write a poem like the 2:30 sun
that shocks you every afternoon as if
it were a hot shower pouring over
your shoulders through your office window so
that you are forced to leave
the poems you have been tending
while you maneuver
the blinds, turn on the lights, resettle.
I wish I could write an inopportune poem,
one that would make you rise complaining
of the heat and the blinding light.
A poem I would write like a fetish;
an undesirable unavoidable poem,
one that would change your life a little like
the Great Vowel Shift did English,
one that would make you want to get up in
the middle of the night to search for things
you didn't know were lost.

THE TRAIN

I travel to know there is still something
between here and there — in order to have
a long way to go. And though at night
the towns look abandoned and dead, I know
there must be life within, for why else
would the train stop? I imagine
someone stirring in her sleep as we ease
into a station, our whistle giving her a dream
of a great ship approaching harbor — a festive
welcome with balloons and streamers.

"Stop and go, stop and go. How can a body
get any rest this-away?" An old woman, black
as the night we are gliding through, mutters behind
me, addressing no one at all.

Out of Jesup at 2 a.m., I notice a porch light
burning. Someone's expected at this house, A young one
out late, and two inside marking the time by our
arrival? Or one alone, waiting for the other,
waiting to make a point lost with the slamming of the
front door? As the tiny speck of light recedes, I am
comforted by the simple patterns
of our lives — how easy it all seems on the move.

"Lord, Lord," she moans and stretches behind me. "Here
we go again. Stop and go, stop and go. My old bones
cain't take much more of this." Gaining power, the train
lurches foward, mimicking her anxiety.
I am traveling south nearly to land's end, memorizing
the country name by name. I'm looking for something
I may have left behind when I knew what each place
called itself. Maps and schedules still summon me like
a child in a game of *hot, hot, hotter — you're
burning.*

Just before dawn, the next stop comes into focus.
In between calls I have lost an hour, and it's
with relief I hear the conductor whisper, "Winter
Haven" over the speaker. His voice is gentle and
promising, for he knows he must not awaken us too
abruptly, "Last call for Winter Haven."

"Thank you, Lord, I'm here at last." She gathers her
many parcels, and grabbing my headrest,
propels herself foward.
As I watch her through my dust-stained window,
a stooped figure dragging her baggage accross the road,
I feel certain she is heading toward one of those
houses that have for miles seemed like nothing more
than Hollywood sets. She will fill it with life like
a balloon. And in other towns along the way others
will do the same, and I will witness it.

Forward. Again my heart adjusts its rhythms
to the engine's. Closing my eyes,
I see a map etched on the vault of my skull,
a bold red X marks the spot where lies the answer to all
my questions. If only I can give it a name.
If the train stops there.

A-1-A

Gulls build their nests on telephone poles,
laying their eggs on the warm terminals.
Could the currents of conversation
become a part of the awakening, subtly changing
the embryos through sounds seeping
into their sacs?
Words of warning of their season: inclement
weather, ships lost at sea, hearts broken
with a click.
The fledgling that fears to trust its instincts
and the wind, wobbling as it perches
over the highway, perhaps listened
too long to the tone of hasty departures, the rise
and fall of voices a warning of the dangers
of flight, the sudden silence a clue
to the message of shells: that nothing lasts.

THE HABIT OF MOVEMENT

Nurtured in the lethargy of the tropics,
the nomadic life did not suit us at first.
We felt like red balloons set adrift
over the wide sky of this new land.
Little by little we lost our will to connect,
and stopped collecting anything heavier
to carry than a wish.
We took what we could from books borrowed
from Greek temples, or holes in the city
walls, returning them hardly handled.

We carried the idea of home on our backs from
house to house, never staying long enough to
learn the secret ways of wood and stone, and
always the blank stare of undraped windows behind
us like the eyes of the unmourned dead.
In time we grew rich in dispossession and
fat with experience.
As we approached but did not touch others,
our habits of movement kept us safe like
a train in motion, nothing could touch us.

LESSON ONE: I WOULD SING

In Spanish, "cantaría" means I would sing,
Cantaría bajo la luna,
I would sing under the moon.
Cantaría cerca de tu tumba,
By your grave I would sing,
Cantaría de una vida perdida,
Of a wasted life I would sing,
If I may, if I could, I would sing.
In Spanish the conditional tense is the tense of dreamers,
of philosophers, fools, drunkards,
of widows, new mothers, small children,
of old people, cripples, saints, and poets.
It is the grammar of expectation and
the formula for hope: *cantaría, amaría, viviría.*
Please repeat after me.

Carolina Cuban

Gustavo Pérez Firmat

Gustavo Pérez Firmat was born March 7, 1949, in Havana, Cuba. He came to the United States with his family in October 1960 and spent his adolescence in Miami. He received his B.A. in English (1972) and M.A. in Spanish (1973) from the University of Miami and was awarded a Ph.D. in Comparative Literature from the University of Michigan in 1979. Pérez Firmat currently teaches Spanish and Spanish American literature at Duke University. He has received numerous awards and grants, including ACLS, NEH, and Guggenheim fellowships. Now a United States citizen, he is married with two children. He resides in Chapel Hill, North Carolina, but he lives in Miami.

Pérez Firmat is the author of several books of literary criticism, including *Idle Fictions: The Hispanic Vanguard Novel* (1982), *Literature and Liminality: Festive Readings in the Hispanic Tradition* (1986), and *In Other Words: Translation and Identity in Modern Cuban Literature* (forthcoming). His poems have appeared in such journals as *The Bilingual Review/La Revista Bilingüe, Linden Lane, Término Magazine, Mariel,* and *Caribbean Review.* He is currently at work on a new collection of poetry, provisionally entitled *Equivocaciones.*

para David (con Miriam)

Vo(I)ces:
Tres fragmentos para un prologo

Dice Rosa que no es realista pasarse el día escuchando a Hansel y Raúl. Yo creo que sí es realista. La falta de realismo yace en creer que es posible, en North Carolina, ser cubano inconsciente, naturalmente. Para ser cubano en North Carolina hay que estar loco. Es una locura que me hace pensar en la furia o manía poética de los griegos (Rosa tiene razón: soy un maniático), y es esa manía la que da lugar a estos poemas schizo, multiplicados por tres y divididos entre el español y el inglés. La esquizofrenia consiste en creer que la realidad es múltiple; la paranoia en creer que es una. Mi locura—esquizo-paranoide—consiste en insistir en la unidad de mis multiplicidades, como en "Turning the Times Tables", como en la tercera parte del poemario, como en este prólogo mismo.

* * *

No deja de sorprenderme que alguien como yo, que llegó a este país a los 11 años y ahora tiene 35, todavía sienta nostalgia hacia lo cubano, todavía se sienta "desterrado". Más de viente años y es como si hubiera llegado ayer, casi: pero de ayer hace ya muchos años. Nostalgia de algo desconocido: por lo tanto, nostalgia/curiosidad—una curiosidad que tiende a la nostalgia y una nostalgia que tiende a la curiosidad. De hecho, me preocupa pensar que algún día al regresar (¿a dónde?) me dé cuenta que lo que siento como nostalgia es sólo curiosidad. Y que me encuentre, entonces, con que lo mío no existe, con que lo propio es lo otro y (por lo tanto) con que yo no soy más (pero tampoco menos) que el espacio marcado por el guión entre Cuban y American, como digo en algún lugar de esta colección.

*   *   *

Por ello se me hace necesario postular una coherencia que tras-
cienda toda fragmentación lingüística y vivencial. Me gustaría
pensar que por debajo o más allá de mi coro de vo(i)ces se puede
escuchar, suave pero insistente, el sonido de una sola voz, el
son de un solo cantante.

Poems in English

The fact that I
am writing to you
in English
already falsifies what I
wanted to tell you.
My subject:
how to explain to you
that I
don't belong to English
though I belong nowhere else,
if not here
in English.

Seeing Snow

Had my father, my grandfather, and his,
had they been asked whether I would ever see snow,
they certainly — in another language —
would have answered,
no. Seeing snow for me
will always mean a slight or not so slight
suspension of the laws of nature.
I was not born to see snow.
I was not meant to see snow.
Even now, snowbound as I've been
all these years,
my surprise does not subside.
What, exactly, am I doing here?
Whose house is this anyway?
For sure one of us has strayed.
For sure someone's lost his way.
This must not be the place.
Where I come from, you know,
it's never snowed:
not once, not ever, not yet.

CHAPEL HILL

Here
we hold our breath
until we're blue
(Carolina blue).
There
we breathe fast
and deep.
Divers in reverse,
we go down for air.
Our lives transpire asth-
matically, by pants and heaves:
chronic asphyxia relieved
by holidays of respiration.

Before I Was a Writer

I used to go
to the Little Professor bookstore
and leaf through southern novels by
Smith or Price or Rubin
and wish I had my own.

El son y la furia:
a bold, breathtaking fictional exploration
of Carolina Cubanness,
the first part set in La Loma del Chaple,
the second in Chapel Hill
(sometimes things translate),
recounting the life and opinions of one — or
several — Gustavo Francisco Tomás Pérez Firmat
from adolescence to adulthood to battered senility
at thirty-two.

But that was before I was a writer.
Now I'm happy
just to think
that tomorrow or the day after
we'll be riding
that same umbilical interstate,
that same life-support highway system,
that same taut arm reaching

back to Miami, mi mami.

LIMEN

We took David back up just when
he was beginning to learn to speak,
to say agua and mamá and galletica.
(Miami es mar y calor y comida.)
Just when he was on the threshold,
at the limen,
perinatal to his past, to me,
we delivered him to y'alls and drawls,
to some place I've never lived in all these years
I have been living there.
(My words are also agua and mamá and galletica
and a few improper names like El Farito,
Chirino, and Dadeland, which is not English
now though it used to be.)
Just as David was beginning to learn to say
the language I breathe in,
we moved him up and inland away
from warmth and water,
knotting his tongue — my tongue — with distance.

WORDS FOR A SOUTHERN SONG

ain't got no mother
tongue
ain't got no father
land
jes had some black-eyed
peas
jes had some country
ham.

I'm jest a Southern
boy
I'm jest a country
man
I keep my belly full
and do the best I
can.

ain't got no mother
tongue
ain't got no father
land
jes had some black-eyed
peas
jes had some country
ham.

CAROLINA BLUES

Everything here is blue.
I've got a blue streak a mile wide
and it won't wash off.
I've complained about it till I'm blue in the face.
I'm seeing blue.
Blue grass in Kentucky is contra natura:
it belongs right here in Carolina.

I hate blue movies, blue boys, blue babies.
To hell with my blue heaven, I don't wanna go.
Vida Blue is my least favorite pitcher
and Bill Blue my least favorite critic.
If you find a true-blue friend, lose him.
I'm not sure what a blue-nose is, but I don't like it.
If God is a tarheel,
he'd have chosen another color.

Give me tritanopia (look it up).
Give me autumn, killer of blues.
Oh for grey skies, yellow leaves, hazel eyes,
black hair, red bricks, white houses.
Oh for all things beautiful and unblue.
Oh for another shot at the spectrum.

CLINTON

for M. S.

Dismal days
evil ways
Hamiltonian humdrum.
Beat it still
up the hill
it'll make you dumb-dumb.

(The exception is a
kirkie named Melissa.)

AFTERPOEM TO "GIRL IN A BIKINI"

I would recant that poem, if I could,
except I never throw out text.
The poem makes me feel a little guilty.
It might be read as sexist.
My wife will not enjoy it.
No one will publish it.

Am I really a pig after all?
And what would poemed nymph opine?

But my poem is so small it fits
inside her bikini. Is so slight
she could swallow it in one gulp.
Is so tiny she'd take it in at a glance
and never feel a thing.

SOME DAY

Go into the bathroom.
Shut the door.
Flip on the bright lights.
Put your glasses on.
Stare straight into the mirror.
And love
Every single dirty little pockmark.

BACON

Let them have motion.
Let them be sensitive.
Leave to them depth of feeling,
subtlety of understanding,
complicated loves.

I'm square
on the side of inarticulate glee.

For me the melody of dishwashers.
For me the mortal grave,
the housefuls, the can of beer,
bacon.

For me the things
that never leave a thing.

SOMETIMES ALL YOU WANT

Sometimes all you want
is the peacefulness of Wednesday nights,
our sofa,
the door half open to hear
the night and exorcise my holy smoke.

No roads or inroads
no ventures or adventures
content with my limitation,
my occasional Armani tie
and Miami.

Sometimes not enough
is good enough.
Sometimes not enough
is all you could ever want.

LAS NAVIDADES DEL 10 DE OCTUBRE

I woke up this morning thinking
it was Christmas day,
mistaking David's tinkering
for toys.

Outside the small pines seemed
incomplete
in their greenness, seemed
colorless where they sat.

The explanation is obvious, even prosaic: anytime the ther-
mometer dips below 65 and the sky is sunny and cloudless, my
body forgets that I no longer live someplace where bright, cool
mornings betoken anything other than autumn.

WAITING GAME

A Cuban has holed himself
up in a sleeping car in Raleigh, North Carolina.
He has been there since Friday and
today it is Sunday.
He has shot and killed his wife.
His daughter, who is nine months old, has dehydrated.
His son, who is four, occupies the hours
asking his mother to wake up.

One Cuban of uncertain origins and destination
has locked himself up
in a sleeping car in a sleeping city
and the swat teams lie in wait.
They wait:
for the son to stop talking
for the father to start shooting
for the dead to start rotting
for the crisis to resolve itself
peacefully and without incident.

SON / SONG

Sometimes I get
the fee
ling that eve
ry word I writ
e deserves a li
ne to itself.
So cha, so cha, so cha
cha
cha
rged with me
aning, with son
g, do they see
m.

HOME

Give a guy a break.
Take him back, let him step
on soil that's his or feels his,
let him have a tongue,
a story, a geography.
Let him not trip back and forth between
bilingualisms,
hyphens,
explanations.
As it is he's a walking-talking bicameral page.
Two hemispheres and neither one likes the other.
Ambidextrous.
Omnipossibilist.
Multivocal.
Let him stop having to translate himself
to himself
endlessly.
Give the guy a break:
crease him, slip him into an envelope,
address it, and let him go.
Home.

Poemas en español

Romance de Coral Gables

Llego a Miami y es otra claridad,
lucidez verde y transparente:
el patio un oleaje de hojas
que inunda las habitaciones.
Florecen los lladrós
flotan las fotografías
se mecen los tenedores
con este norte que me trae el sur
de la Florida.
El televisor es un barco de velas verdes,
cada lámpara es un mástil:
tallos que retoñan igual que yo,
clorofílico en este mar de vida.

Verde que me quiero verde
(pero mi Granada está en Coral Gables).

Mi madre cuando nos visita

Mi madre cuando nos visita
tiñe todo
de familiaridad:
viste de verde y mar
mi jardín de tierra adentro
(cuando ella está mi casa es carabela),
imparte el color del cariño
a estos raros rojos otoñales
y bajo sus pisadas las hojas
crujen amorosamente.

El aire se hace respiración.
La soledad se vuelve habitable.
Lo extraño torna hogareño
cada otoño
mi madre cuando nos visita.

MINIMA ELEGIA BILINGÜE

Morirse de cáncer
en el exilio
es ser invadido y conquistado
por la sustancia misma de la separación.

El cuerpo extraño — foreign body —
nos corroe con su extranjeridad.
Cada célula maligna se aloja
en el útero o en un pulmón
como un pedacito de alguien que no soy yo,
alguien que habla en inglés y detesta el café con leche,
y a cuyas costumbres — irremisiblemente —
terminaré por convertirme.

NOCHE DE RHONDA

¿Y qué se ha hecho del Ecuanil,
calmante predilecto del primer exilio,
sustituido ahora por las insípidas pastillitas de Valium
(5 milígramos) o el inagotable Librax manufacturado
especialmente para la gente — como yo — no sólo hyper
o nerviosa o asustada sino además con cagalera?
(Ecuanil: noches de insomnio de mi madre,
fruto vedado, amor imposible, pasaporte de la madurez.)
Y si tienes suerte y conoces al boticario
consigues el inigualable Atarax
(10 milígramos): Nirvana de la Pequeña Habana.
Atarax que tumba, te hace tierra en el destierro,
te hace olvidar el valium (ave atque valium)
te hace olvidar a tu madre (ave atque mami)
te hace olvidarlo todo, todo, todo, todorov
(¿de dónde tzvetan los cantantes?)
y te hunde te hunde te hunde te hunde
en un letargo largo, tupido y sin fin.

THE SOUTHERN PART OF HEAVEN

A César Cauce, muerto por el KKK
el tres de noviembre de 1979 en
una calle de Greensboro, N.C.

Qué privilegio morir en North Carolina.
De la vida a la muerte, un pasito nada más.
De la muerte a la tumba, otro mínimo pasito.
Y de la tumba al cielo, nada.

Por eso digo que derrumbarse de un tiro
en North Carolina
es caer de cabeza en el cielo.
Y al caer ver a San Pedro esperándote,
en cualquier calle de cualquier pueblo,
con una sábana blanca.

MIDDLEBURY, VERMONT

A la entrada, un cementerio.
A la salida, otro cementerio
(ya me explico el *bury*).
Pero en el medio, ¿qué?
¿En medio de qué, precisamente, está Middlebury?
(Inteligencia, dame la cosa
que explique el nombre inexacto.)

¿En medio del monte? Quizá.
¿En el culo del mundo? Posiblemente.
Primera definición provisional:
Middlebury: monte/culo/cementerio.

¿Qué hace un cubano en Middlebury?
¿Qué hace un cubano en medio
de este medio sin medio?
¿Qué me hago, Dios mío, sin remedio
en Middlebury,
medio muerto, muerto y medio?

I come not to praise Caesar but to Middlebury him.
I come not to Middlebury but to Muddlebury.
I come to Muddlebury.
Segunda definición provisional:
Muddlebury.

Definición definitiva:
Middlebury: Muddlebury:
monte/culo/cementerio.

CUBANITA DESCUBANIZADA

Cubanita descubanizada,
quién te pudiera recubanizar.
Quién supiera devolverte
el ron y la palma,
el alma y el son.

Cubanita descubanizada,
tú que pronuncias todas las eses
y dices ómnibus y autobús,
quién te pudiera
quién te supiera
si te quisieras recubanizar.

EL FARITO DE MIAMI

> Oye, Tere,
> esto sí es vida.
> (oído en Crandon Park)

Primera instantánea

El Duque de Rivas, redivivo,
tirado en una toalla de playa
con trusa de nadador — negra y estrecha —
y el radio portátil en la Super Q,
el sonido de Miami *(mai-a-mi)*.
Tiene 43 años, panza,
y discretamente rascabuchea
a una niña de quince
que se acaba de soltar los tirantes de la trusa
para tostarse mejor.
Su única herida — menos que mortal —
se la proporcionó
un eminente galeno cubano-americano
al sacarle la vesícula,
tan llena de arenilla
como lo están ahora los lentes de sus espejuelos.

(El Duque es miope
y se llama Angel González.)

Segunda instantánea

Aquí concebí mi tipología de la musa:
minimusa — no está mal;
mesomusa — está buena;
maximusa — requetebuena, enferma,
como aquélla de la trusa vieja
y el cuerpo por estrenar.

Tercera instantánea

Los dos salvavidas
—uno cubano, el otro no—
se dicen cosas, pelean.
This is your last day on the job, buddy,
dice el americano.
You wanna make something of it,
You wanna make something of it,
dice y repite el cubano.
El americano (rubio, of course)
le saca media cabeza.

Cuarta instantánea

El mar se hizo para los niños
que no saben nadar.
Nosotros, los demás, somos lápidas navegables,
túmulos que se cruzan,
carne muerta en aguas vivas.
Sólo los niños,
los que no saben nadar,
se confunden con las olas
intiman con la espuma
conocen el elemento.
Sólo los niños
saben hacer del mar
otra morada.

DIA DE LOS PADRES EN CHAPEL HILL

Hoy celebro mi enajenación
multiplicada por dos.
Hoy celebro esos extraños, mis hijos,
en quienes no me reproduzco.
Celebro todo lo que no soy yo
y me rodea
todo lo que soy yo
y me falta.

También celebro la geografía de mi cerebro
escindido en hemisferios,
mi corazón ventrílocuo y mis lenguas.
Celebro, en fin, lo de siempre:
    mi ansia de mar
    mi sed de arena
    mi tristeza tropical
    la latitud y longitud de mis poemas.

PAGINA EN BLANCO .

Página en blanco,
estas palabras son para ti.
Las inscribo no porque tenga algo que decir
(yo nunca he dicho nada a nadie, igual que tú),
sino sencillamente para que te sientas
menos sola y desolada
menos pálida y triste,
para que te acompañen éstas mis gráficas caricias,
ávidas como hormigas en un terrón de azúcar.

VIVIR SIN HISTORIA

He viajado poco, he vivido menos.
No se explica este cansancio y sin embargo
estoy cansado.

Desde mi margen contemplo
a los hombres-pararrayos, a los hombres-volcán,
a los hombres-liebre.
Contemplo al héroe de última hora
y al mártir del momento.
Contemplo las inmolaciones, los sacrificios,
las bellas catástrofes que harán historia.

Yo no tengo historia
y sin embargo estoy cansado.

Cansado de la historia, entre otras cosas,
y de las inmolaciones
y de los sacrificios
y de las bellas catástrofes
y sobre todo de los héroes
y sobre todo de los mártires.

Pudrirse de grima en una cárcel puede
ser mala suerte o mala leche.
Mas ya cansa tanta tragedia:
tanta viuda atrincherada en su luto,
tanto hijo huérfano,
tanto exilio, tanto padecer.

La orfandad es bonita pero también cansa.
El dolor de los demás es bonito pero también cansa.
Atención bayameses:
bajad las voces
detened la marcha
deponed las banderas
y las bayonetas.

Traigo un secreto que confiaros:
vivir sin historia es vivir.

POEMA DE AMOR AL GENERAL SANDINO

Sandino dame un besito
no seas tan ariscón
un beso largo y dulzón
beso de generalito.

Oye yo me permito
hacerte esta petición
porque tengo la ilusión
de robarte un cariñito.

Sandino no seas malito
Sandino no seas malón:
escucha mi petición
Sandino, dame un besito.

BLOOMINGTON, ILLINOIS

Ni sé en qué idioma escribirte,
blooming town donde nada nunca nadie
florece ha florecido o florecerá.
En el corazón de ésta casi mi tierra no hay flores.
Pero sí—compensación—rubias, trigueñas y pelirrojas
casi mejor que flores.

Mariposa: flor que vuela.
Poeta: también vuela pero no es flor ni mariposa.
En Bloomington tampoco hay poetas.
Pero sí—compensación—un muchacho que dibuja pingüinos
tan obsoletos como el cine en blanco y negro.

¿Quién me hubiera dicho
que en Bloomington, Illinois,
corazón de ésta casi mi tierra
iba a resucitar el pingüino?

OYE BROTHER

Oye brother. Tú eres mi hermano, claro.
Tú eres mi sangre, claro.
No te olvidé, claro.
Pero son veinte años,
pero ya es otro mundo,
pero somos distintos, claro,
aunque somos iguales.

Oye brother. Tú eres mi tierra, claro,
pero mucho ha cambiado,
aunque tú eres my brother, claro,
aunque somos cubanos.

Pero. Claro. Aunque.
Aunque. Pero. Claro.

                          Miami, verano de 1980

Entre hermanos

Hermano, yo a ti no te conozco
y tú a mí no me leerás.
Nos separan tu indiferencia y mi cansancio
(o tu cansancio y mi indiferencia, da igual).
Nos separan tus palabras y mis pausas,
tus júbilos y mis vacilaciones.
La cotidianidad, que debiera unirnos,
nos separa también:
tantos años de convivencia sin confluencia.
Porque aquí, entre hermanos,
no existe ni siquiera un camino,
ningún tránsito compartido, ningún sendero por compartir.
Aquí, entre hermanos,
nadie nunca ha dicho nada a nadie;
aquí, sencillamente, no ha pasado nada.
Por eso te digo ahora, hermano que no escuchas
(hermano que no existes),
que yo ti no te conozco
y que tú a mí no me leerás.

Matriz y margen

A Roberto Valero

Roberto: joven hermano mayor
en la poesía y en la historia:
reconozco mi déficit de acontecer.
En tus palabras hay matriz,
en las mías, margen.
En tu acento hay espesor y alarma,
en el mío, reminiscencia.

Y sin embargo reclamo un turno y una voz
en nuestra historia.
Reclamo *marcar* en la cola
de ese ilustre cocodrilo inerte
que nos devora en la distancia.
Reclamo la pertinencia y el mar.

También es matriz mi margen.
Mi recuerdo se espesa como tu acento.
Yo también llevo el cocodrilo a cuestas.
Y digo que sus aletazos verdes me baten
incesantemente.
Y digo que me otorgan la palabra
y el sentido.
Y digo que sin ellos no sería lo que soy
y lo que no soy:
una brisa de ansiedad y recuerdo
soplando hacia otra orilla.

PROVOCACIONES

> ¿Cómo puede seguir uno viviendo
> con dos lenguas, dos casas, dos nostalgias
> dos tentaciones, dos melancolías?
> —Heberto Padilla, "Postcard to USA"

Y yo te respondo, Heberto, talmúdicamente:
¿cómo no seguir viviendo con dos
lenguas casas nostalgias tentaciones melancolías?
Porque no puedo amputarme una lengua
ni tumbar una casa
ni enterrar una melancolía.
Quisiera, al contrario,
singularizar lo indivisiblemente dividido,
hacer de dos grandes ojos una sola mirada.

Other poems / Otros poemas

Son-Sequence

Call these poems a son-sequence:
Son as plural being.
Son as rumba beat.
Son as progeny.
Son, fueron, serán.
Son, danzón, guaracha.
Son, his father's son.
Is he?

CAROLINA CUBAN (I)

Carolina Cuban I'd always thought
was to be a book or poem about me.
But tonight
in the OB section of
Memorial Hospital,
after fifteen hours of Rosa's labor,
two shots of Demerol,
the epidural and several valiums,
I know that Carolina Cuban
will be you, David or Miriam.

You will be the true tarheel cubiche,
the real mixed thing.
(I'm not mixed, just mixed up.)
But you will be a rare
Carolina blue plate of
          lechón con grits;
          iced tea and tasajo:
coño, with a southern drawl.

You, Miriam or David,
first of la raza cósmica,
right here in Chapel Hill, North Carolina,
on June 10, 1981
at one o'clock in the morning.

CAROLINA CUBAN (II)

con Jorge Olivares

mami papi tío
nena agua jugo cereal
pollo galletica papita cake
helado guauguau baño
niño niña gato
se cayó

hello yes
adiós byebye
ahí aquí

pipi caca talco más
carro casa vamos no hay
quién es
hoja guagua ya
baila zapato reloj

baby
why
se acabó

Chapel Hill, diciembre de 1982

TURNING THE TIMES TABLES

> I am the sum total of my language.
> —Charles Sanders Peirce

¿Y si soy más de uno, Peirce?
¿Y si soy dos,
o tres
o—como diría David—
un millón?
¿En qué momento, en qué participio del mundo
se convierte tu suma en mi resta, Peirce?

I am what is left
after the subtraction of my languages.
I am the division that resists
the multiplication of my languages.
I am the number that won't square,
the figure you can't figure,
the remainder of my languages.

One into two
won't go.
You into tú
won't go.
Yo into you
won't go.
I into yo
won't go.
Nothing into nada
won't go.

Split the difference.
Split the atom.
Split.
I still won't go.

Some people
just
don't add
up.

Bilingual Blues

Soy un ajiaco de contradicciones.
I have mixed feelings about everything.
Name your tema, I'll hedge;
name your cerca, I'll straddle it
like a cubano.

I have mixed feelings about everything.
Soy un ajiaco de contradicciones.
Vexed, hexed, complexed,
hyphenated, oxygenated, illegally alienated,
psycho soy, cantando voy:
You say tomato,
I say tu madre;
You say potato,
I say Pototo.
Let's call the hole
un hueco, the thing
a cosa, and if the cosa goes into the hueco,
consider yourself en casa,
consider yourself part of the family.

Soy un ajiaco de contradicciones,
un potaje de paradojas:
a little square from Rubik's Cuba
que nadie nunca acoplará.
(Cha-cha-chá.)

Filosofias del no

I am most me when I mumble.
A native mumbler of two languages,
I have mastered the art of imprecision
and of indecision, haltingly.

No me podrán quitar mi dolorido sentir,
this little pain in my corazoncito
that makes me stutter
barbarismos y barbaridades.

Por example:
el cubano-americano es un estar que no sabe dónde es.
Por example:
el cubano-americano se nutre de lo que le falta.

Cubano-americano: ¿dónde soy?
Soy la marca entre un *no* y un *am*:
filósofo del no
filósofo del ah, no
filósofo del anón
(que seguramente nunca habré probado).

Cubano-americano: ¿dónde soy?
son que se fue de Cuba
corazón que dejé enterrado
rinconcito de mi tierra
pedacito de cielo: ¿dónde soy?
Un extraviado
Un faccioso
Un inconforme
Un dividido
cuba: no
america: no

¿Dónde soy?
Sólo sé que nadar sé.
Sólo sé que tengo sed.
Dame un trago.
Dame un break.
Dame un besito en el — ah, no —
y hazme olvidar mis penas.

CAROLINA CUBAN (III)

An I
For an I
For an I–95

Acknowledgments *(continued)*

Other poems by Judith Ortiz Cofer included in this volume previously appeared in *Affinities*, Vol. 3, No. 1 (1980): "Walking to Church" and "Grace Stands in Line for Saturday Confession"; *The Florida Arts Gazette*, Vol. 3, Issue 9 (1980): "Baptism at La Misión"; *Hispanics in the United States: An Anthology of Creative Literature*, Vol. II, eds. Francisco Jiménez and Gary D. Keller (Ypsilanti, MI: Bilingual Press, 1980): "My Father in the Navy" and "En mis ojos no hay días"; *Kalliope*, Vol. 4, No. 3 (1982): "Lesson One: I Would Sing"; *The Louisville Review*, No. 12 (1982): "Housepainter"; *New Collage*, Vol. 14, No. 2 (1983): "She Has Been a Long Time Dying"; *New Letters*, Vol. 50, No. 1 (1983): "Room at the Empire"; *New Mexico Humanities Review*, Vol. 4, No. 1 (1981): "Latin Women Pray"; *Nosotras: Latina Literature Today*, eds. Ma. del Carmen Boza, Beverly Silva, and Carmen Valle (Binghamton, NY: Bilingual Press, 1986): "The Other" and "They Say"; *Orphic Lute*, Spring Issue (1984): "Treasure"; *The Panhandler*, No. 13 (1983): "We Are All Carriers"; *The Pawn Review*, Vol. 15 (1984): "Because My Mother Burned Her Legs in a Freak Accident"; *Poets On: Barriers*, Vol. 8, No. 1 (1984): "Meditation on My Hands"; *Prairie Schooner*, Vol. 59, No. 1 (1985): "The Woman Who Was Left at the Altar" and "Claims"; *South Florida Poetry Review*, Vol. 1, No. 2 (1984): "Closed Casket"; *Southern Poetry Review*, Vol. 23, No. 2 (1983): "In Yucatan" and "Returning from the Mayan Ruins"; and Vol. 24, No. 2 (1984): "La tristeza"; *Tendril*, Seventh Anniversary Issue, No. 19-20 (1985): "Letter from a Caribbean Island."

Several poems in this book were also first published as part of a limited edition chapbook entitled *The Native Dancer* (Bourbonnais, IL: Pteranodon Press, 1981).

Gustavo Pérez Firmat and the editors wish to thank Barry Levine, Editor, *Caribbean Review*, for permission to reprint "Bilingual Blues" and "Turning the Times Tables," which first appeared in *Caribbean Review*, Vol. XV, No. 3.

Several poems by Pérez Firmat originally appeared in *The Bilingual Review/La Revista Bilingüe:* "The Southern Part of Heaven," "Oye Brother," "Bloomington, Illinois," and "Poema de amor al General Sandino," in Vol. VII, No. 3 (Sept.-Dec. 1980); "Carolina Cuban (I)" and "Home," in Vol. IX, No. 2 (May-Aug. 1982); and "Before I Was a Writer" and "Seeing Snow," in Vol. XI, No. 3 (Sept.-Dec. 1984).